This Little Tiger book belongs to:

_____

_____

_____

To my
amazing family
~RT

For Tilia
~PH

CATERPILLAR BOOKS
An imprint of the Little Tiger Group
www.littletiger.co.uk • 1 Coda Studios,
189 Munster Road, London SW6 6AW
Imported into the EEA by Penguin Random House Ireland,
Morrison Chambers, 32 Nassau Street, Dublin D02 YH68
This edition published in 2021
First published in 2020 • Text by Patricia Hegarty
Text copyright © Caterpillar Books Ltd 2020
Illustrations copyright © Rotem Teplow 2020
A CIP catalogue record for this book
is available from the British Library
All rights reserved • Printed in China
ISBN: 978-1-83891-362-5
CPB/1400/2209/0622
2 4 6 8 10 9 7 5 3

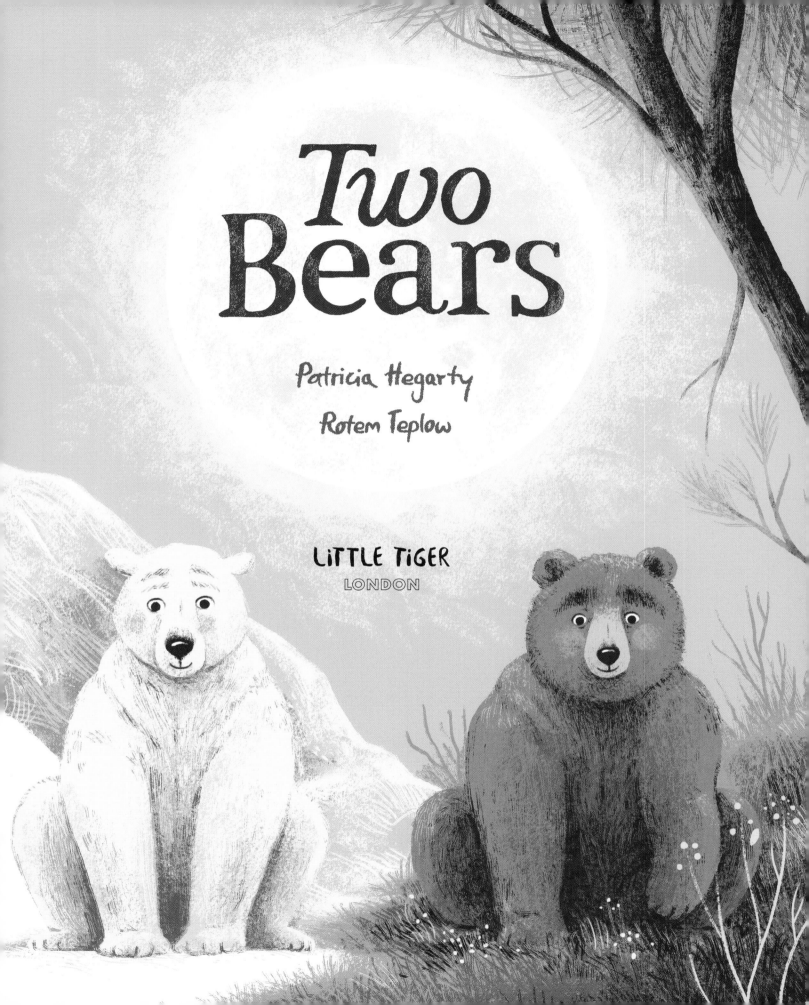

# Two Bears

Patricia Hegarty

Rotem Teplow

LITTLE TIGER
LONDON

This is the story of two bears,
who lived many, many miles
from each other in two
very different worlds.

Polar Bear lived
in the **frozen** lands
of the Arctic.

Grizzly Bear lived
in the **heart** of the
northern forests.

Polar Bear
spent her days
**diving** and **swimming**
to the depths of the
icy blue ocean
in search
of food.

Grizzly Bear's hunting
grounds stretched through
pine woods and clear
**sparkling** rivers.

They may have lived far apart but, when night fell, the two bears would rest beneath the same **starry** skies, gazing up at the same **silvery** moon.

A time came when strangers
invaded Grizzly Bear's world.
Fires **raged** through the forest
as man sought to tame nature.

Meanwhile, Polar Bear's home was in peril as the weather became warmer and the ice caps began to melt away.

The lives of the two bears were
soon to change forever as they were
forced to seek a place of safety.

And so the journeys began.

Polar Bear turned her face
determinedly to the south.

Grizzly Bear began a gruelling trek
northwards in search of food.

The weeks passed and the two bears journeyed
on through snow and wind, sunshine and rain.

They grew thinner and thinner as food became scarce,
but the bears knew that they must stay strong to survive...

And then, one day,
as the bears were close to despair,

a wonderful
thing happened.

The two bears from two different
worlds came face to face.

Was this to be their
new home?

The bears quickly learnt that
they had much in common despite
the different colours of their fur.

The things that they shared were
far more important: both craved
food and shelter and to live
their lives in peace
and harmony.

And so, two bears from different
worlds made a life together.

With the arrival of spring,
two bears became **three** and
the family was complete.

Their baby bear looked a little
like each of them and he saw no
difference between them.

He knew no
other home and
his heart was full.

This was his family.

# Bears on the Brink

### Polar Bears

 Polar bears live in the Arctic.
They were listed as a threatened species in the US in 2008. The main threat to the polar bear's survival is the loss of its sea-ice habitat, as the ice melts due to climate change.

The Southern Beaufort Sea population of polar bears has halved since the 1980s, with only about 900 bears remaining.

In some areas, female polar bears are choosing to make their 'maternity dens' (a snow cave in which they give birth) on land rather than ice. But, human activity, such as drilling for gas and oil, can disturb the bears and force them to abandon the dens too early, putting their cubs at risk.

### Grizzly Bears

 The main threat to grizzly bears also comes from the destruction of their natural habitat. The grizzly bear population has had to adapt as cities and transport links have been built across its territories.

Climate change has adversely affected some of the grizzly bear's food sources, such as white bark pine seeds. This has sometimes led to grizzlies seeking out new ways to find food – including scavenging from human rubbish bins.

### Baby Bears!

 In the past, the habitats of the polar bear and the grizzly bear remained separate, but as they have been forced to adapt, polar bears have travelled further south, while some grizzlies have ventured northward.

As a result, there is now a new bear on the block! Half polar bear and half grizzly, this new hybrid has been called either a 'pizzly bear' or a 'grolar bear'. Others have suggested the name 'nanulak', derived from the Inuit names for the two bears.

# What Can We Do?
*It's not too late to help the bears...*

### Waste Not, Want Not!
We can help by not wasting precious resources – reusing shopping bags and recycling household items is a great start.

### We Are What We Eat!
Buying locally sourced produce and eating less meat and dairy will help to reduce our 'carbon footprint' (the amount of damaging carbon dioxide released into the atmosphere by farming animals and food transport).

### Walk, Don't Ride!
We don't always need to jump in the car – if we can walk or use public transport instead, we will help to reduce harmful 'carbon emissions'.